RebuildingBooks
For Divorce and Beyond

101 Little Instructions for Surviving Your Divorce

A No-Nonsense Guide to the Challenges at Hand

Barbara J. Walton

Impact Publishers®, Inc.
ATASCADERO, CALIFORNIA

ATTENTION ORGANIZATIONS AND CORPORATIONS:
This book is available at quantity discounts on bulk purchases for educational, business, or sales promotional use. For further information, please contact Impact Publishers, P.O. Box 6016, Atascadero, California 93423-6016.
Phone: 1-800-246-7228.

Library of Congress Cataloging-in-Publication Data

Walton, Barbara J.
   101 little instructions for surviving your divorce : a no-nonsense
guide to the challenges at hand / Barbara J. Walton.
       p. cm.
  Includes bibliographical references and index.
  ISBN 1-886230-24-2
  1. Divorced people--United States Life skills guides. 2. Divorced
parents---Unted States Life skills guides. 3. Divorce--United
States Miscellanea.   I. Title.   II. Title: One hundred one little
instructions for surviving your divorce.
  HQ834.W373   1999
  306.89--dc21   99-32600
                                          CIP

Impact Publishers and colophon are registered trademarks of Impact Publishers, Inc.

Cover design by John Magee, San Luis Obispo, California
Printed in the United States of America on acid-free paper
Published by ***Impact ◈ Publishers,® Inc.***
POST OFFICE BOX 6016
ATASCADERO, CALIFORNIA 93423-6016
WWW.IMPACTPUBLISHERS.COM

For Mary Lee, who gave me permission.

Contents

Foreword

Acknowledgements

No successful project is ever accomplished by one person alone. I'd like to credit the struggles my clients have passed through as teaching me many lessons I have been able to share here, and wish them the best as they move onward. Thanks to William Pineo, Esq. for his words of wisdom, as well as the many judges and hearing officers with whom I have worked.

Special thanks to George Wright, my father, who has done divorce recovery work for years and provided valuable insights; Roberta Kear, John Haynes, Gina Chatfield for their review and honest comments, and everyone who has encouraged this endeavor.

Foreword

After twelve years of practice in the family law field, as often as I think I've seen everything, there's always some new case which is a revelation. Unfortunately, what usually surprises me are not the facts of the case, but the extent to which the parties either destroy each other or themselves in the process.

At its best, a divorce is a legal untangling of the ties between a husband and wife. The *legal divorce* will set the financial and custodial requirements, including division of property. The *emotional divorce* will force the partners to admit they aren't "the one" who fulfills all their hopes and dreams, and move the partners beyond dependency on each other. The *community divorce* will redefine how each of the spouses relates to their friends, family and community. The *co-parental divorce* will deal with each parent's loss of control over the children and the time the other parent spends with the children.

None of these are easy, and it is thanks to the many clients I've guided through these processes that I am able to share these "Instructions" with you. I've learned from their struggles, as they have, and now you can, too.

The intention of this book is not to be a sit-down read. I suggest you read some portion of the book, then think about what's been said, and compare it with your own situation. Not everything will apply to your case, and you may find you have more specific questions than the answers provided here. But common sense and practical thinking will surely lead you to your healthiest conclusion.

1
Divorce

Tips and pointers to make the process easier

1

Divorce is not an event; it's a process. Whether it takes three weeks, three months, or three years, nothing will be solved immediately. Take a deep breath and relax as much as you can.

2

There are steps most people go through in the process of a separation and divorce, similar to the steps in the grieving process after a death: denial, anger, grief, acceptance. A person in the denial stage can go through the motions of filing paperwork, but will not be "ready" for a divorce until the steps are completed.

Often partners do not progress through these steps at the same speed or same time. A spouse who has been secretly planning to leave the marriage for some time may have gone through all four stages before the spouse who's left behind becomes aware there's a problem. The process should and can wait until the second spouse works through his or her feelings.

4

Two issues should be handled expeditiously:

    1) You and the children must be safe.

    2) You and the children must have a roof over your head and food on the table.

These are survival questions. Once they're provided for, the rest can take as long as you need.

5

Unless a survival issue is at hand, there's no reason to rush to file a divorce. Often there is no advantage to filing "first." Wait until you feel you can handle it, both financially and psychologically.

6

The longer you have been invested in a marriage, the more thought you should give to working to save it, if that's possible. Marriage counseling, if both parties put their hearts into it, often helps. If there is no hope, either because of misconduct or a lack of love, then you should give some thought to ending the relationship expeditiously. Life isn't a dress rehearsal. You don't have the opportunity to do it again, if you regret being unhappy for ten or twenty years by failing to take action.

You can always "win" a divorce the hard way, cutting and slashing, with a winner-take-all attitude. It will cost you a lot more, both in money and mental health. Will it really be worth it ten years from now?

8

There are some people who can have a "friendly" divorce. There are some people who can't, because the facts are too unpleasant.

9

If you're one of the former, work through your settlement and go on with your lives. If you're one of the latter, deal with the abuse or the adultery or the immediate problem as distantly as you can, and try to settle the rest. No one will expect you to be best friends. But you have the ability to take control of whatever issues are not too painful and work through them. Empower yourself.

10

When you're going through a divorce, everyone will have war stories and advice for you. What you really need to know is that each legal process is different, because the facts of each person's existence are never identical. Just because Joe or Sandy at your shop pays $100 a month in child support or got the house doesn't mean you will. Just because they didn't, doesn't mean you won't.

Laws change; the way people got divorced twenty years ago may be totally irrelevant. Ask a legal professional for the straight story, based on current law in your state.

12

Some people really get emotionally invested in concern about their partner's new love. You might take some comfort in the fact that rebound relationships hardly *ever* work.

13

Be aware that once you involve the court in your life, the rules change. Husbands and wives who may have cheated on their taxes for years find that one may use it in court against the other. Parents who may have smoked marijuana together the whole time they were married may get turned in to the police now that a custody action is pending. Casual baby-sitting arrangements which were fine when the parties were together come under fire. Think about possible consequences before you act.

2
Custody

Looking out for the person whose interest is the most important and least represented in your separation — your child

14

The trend toward mediation of custody matters is a good one. It takes the power from the judge and the attorneys and gives it back to you. After all, who is better qualified to determine what should happen to your children?

15

Many states now require some form of joint parenting, acknowledging current studies showing it is important to a child's development to have good interaction with both mother and father.

16

If your child enjoys a good relationship with both parents, be grateful! Even if you and your spouse can't get along with each other, the love bond your child forms with each of you will help shape future relationships for the rest of his or her life. Don't allow your hurt feelings to damage your child's future.

Don't communicate about adult divorce and custody matters through your child. If you can't talk face-to-face with your spouse, try talking on the telephone. If you can't talk over the telephone, write letters. Use the "Dragnet" method: "Just the facts, ma'am." You don't have to be warm, just polite.

18

Visit your children, even if the custodial parent makes it difficult. Your absence leaves the message: "You're not loved." And you can't wait to rebuild the relationship after the children turn 18, because the damage is done by then.

19

There are ways in every state to enforce visitation orders. Take advantage of them, even if it doesn't seem worth the trouble. Penalties can include fines and even jail time. Your child has the right to see you, and you have the power to enforce your child's rights. Use it!

20

Be there on time, whether picking up your child or dropping off. There's nothing sadder than a little face pressed up against the glass waiting for his cherished time with mom or dad, and that parent not appearing. If you'll be late, call and let them know. If you're not able to come, call and make other arrangements. Your courtesy is also an investment in good relations with the other parent, which may pay off in greater flexibility in the future.

21

A child is not a fork or spoon or automobile with a title to be transferred to one parent or the other. She is not "mine," she is "ours." Whoever her father or mother is, that person is someone you chose to have sexual relations with so you could create that child. It doesn't change anything if you're unhappy about that later. At the time when it was important, you selected that person as worthy. You have to live with that choice.

Keep in mind as your children get older, particularly in the teen years, even if both parents were at home, they would spend less and less time with you and more with their friends and a part-time job, as they flirt with the adult world. Any custody and visitation order should allow the child some time for these activities, and parents can consult with their teen to find what time is most convenient. In two or three years, remember, that "child" won't need either of you, except for occasional meals and laundry.

23

One of the issues a child finds most difficult is Mommy or Daddy's new "friend." While you may want to date, once your separation is official, it's difficult to explain to a child why you're still married to his other parent, but sleeping with someone else. The child can also become confused about his loyalties, especially if the new friend is someone he enjoys being with. Many experts recommend a trial period for you and your new love of six months or upwards before you introduce him or her into the child's life.

Make sure your new love is someone you're going to keep around for awhile. A child who learns to love a new parental figure can be hurt if that person is suddenly gone. If there is a series of friends who come and go, the child most likely learns the lesson that it is painful to love people, because they only leave. She may then adapt this lesson to her own life and refuse to love anyone, to prevent herself being hurt. Is this the kind of legacy you want to give your child?

25

Parents can do a lot to reassure children who might be nervous about visitation. Time with Mom or Dad should be anticipated happily by the child. You, as a parent, can do a lot to keep the kids excited about their time by keeping a calendar, so they know how many days till it's time to go, and reminding them about the fun activities they do with their other parent. Children read a lot from your attitude ---- if you can be positive, they will, too.

26

While it is important to allow your children, especially if they're older, some input into decisions which are going to impact their lives, sometimes well-meaning parents can put too much pressure on the kids by demanding to know "what they want." If the child has a ready opinion, take it at face value. If the child is reluctant to express an opinion, honor his or her privacy and guilt over torn loyalties and proceed without it. After all, your child is still a child; the bottom-line responsibilities belong to the adults.

Sometimes we find that, sadly, neither parent is really suited or capable of taking care of the children. If your attorney suggests some parenting classes or family counseling, you shouldn't take it as a personal attack, even though your nerves may be strained to the max. He or she has handled many cases and knows which cards will play well in your hand in court.

The areas the court will look at in terms of deciding custody revolve around the relationship of the parent and child. This includes such issues as the amount of time spent with the child daily, and the quality of that time; the parent's work schedule and availability for the child, the parent's past behavior toward the child, and the parents' weaknesses and strengths.

29

The court will review its information and make a decision for you, based on a few hours' informational testimony. I wonder: How can the judge or custody mediator possibly know you or the child in that amount of time?

30

Sometimes there are two parents, equally committed to their children, whose schedules are similar, each has a special activity with the children (Mom with Girl Scouts, Dad coaches soccer), both have similar incomes, and both want to be primary custodian of the children. If you've put this decision in the judge's lap, you'd better hope your judge has the wisdom of Solomon, because those kids' future depends on it.

3
Mental Health

Why it's important to take care of yourself and your children, relieving stress and expecting tantrums

Why is it we can be friendly and smile at perfect strangers, or the checkout girl and bag boy at the grocery store, but we can't even use ordinary civility to a person we used to love deeply?

32

In my practice, I've found that many clients who have an ugly, bitter divorce discover several years later that their long-term health has been affected, either by cancer or some other debilitating disease. I'm sure there's no scientific study linking these two factors, but it would make sense that marinating in poison would damage the human system. Get some counseling. Learn to let go of some of the bitterness. Building yourself up should be at least as important as tearing someone else down.

33

Because the legal system can work slowly, it's important to find positive ways to work off the stress that will inevitably occur. Walk. Bike. Paint. Sculpt. Take up martial arts, which combines a disciplined mind with a fit body. Better yet, do these things with your kids once in awhile. They'll appreciate the time you're sharing.

34

Find activities for your child to help expand his outlook. Wouldn't it be better for him to remember the year he was seven as the year he learned to dive or hit his first home run, instead of the year his parents were divorced?

35

Your children will act out their frustration, hurt and pain, and probably at a time when you are feeling like you need someone to take care of *you* instead. Being prepared for it is your best defense.

36

The child's age will have an impact on the form of the outburst, because there are different ages where a child relates better to her father or her mother, or in the teen years, with neither. A counselor can provide you some generic advice on how to best handle the child's reaction, even if you don't provide the child with counseling directly.

37

It's my experience that the group hardest-hit are the budding adolescents. They're old enough to understand some of the adult perspectives, but not fully equipped to handle and process an additional, huge variable in their world, already unbalanced by hormones and other problems of adolescence. Keep an eye on them. If you lose them now, they're old enough to be seriously hurt and do great damage in their turn.

38

Children are intimately involved in your divorce, no matter how you try to protect them. Rule # 1: *Assure them the breakup is not their fault.* A child may internalize misplaced guilt and not share it with you, so encourage an open discussion.

39

Rule # 2. *Never lie to the children about what's going on.* It's better to say nothing than not to be honest. (But you don't have to tell them *everything*, either.)

Rule #3: *Don't put the children in the middle.* Don't make them carry bills or other communications back and forth between the parents. Their time with the parent shouldn't be clouded by his or her unhappiness over what was sent. This is a matter where the parents must develop a good system for communicating between themselves.

Rule #4: It is appropriate to *include the children,* particularly the older ones, *in some discussions about what's happening* or what might happen, and in some decision-making that will affect them. If they don't want to participate, that's fine; they are still children and you are the parent. But some children welcome the opportunity to have a little input, just as you would.

42

If you feel the edges of your life slipping away from you, resolve to become more organized. Keep your legal paperwork in order, keep a journal or notebook where all your observations and experiences are listed together, and start keeping track of when the bills are due, and then are paid. There are many parts of a separation which are out of your control ---- begin with the details of your own life, where you do have some power, and grow from there.

43

Many organizations offer support in the form of divorce recovery workshops or single parent groups. There are also a number of excellent single parent and divorce information Web Sites on the Internet where you can "chat" with other people working through the same feelings and circumstances. Take advantage of the support ---- these are people who know what you're going through.

44

Get plenty of sleep when you can. There will be times you are so stressed you won't be able to sleep at night; this is natural under the circumstances, and you shouldn't worry about that ---- you're probably worrying about enough things! Even if that means you have a catnap each afternoon before the kids get home from school, it's a time for rest. Take advantage of it.

45

Stress and disquiet consume vitamins and nutrients. One of the best things you can do for yourself and your family is to make sure you eat well, observing the proper diet. Take a multivitamin with extra B vitamins for stress, and eat enough fruits and vegetables so your body works well. It's something you still have under your control, and letting yourself get run down will only lead to more difficulties in the long run.

46

In the same vein, exercise will help relieve stress. Whether you take an aerobics class, work with a video at home or just talk a walk every day, the activity should help recharge you and loosen tension's grip on your body.

47

Don't let others tell you what you're feeling. Friends or family might assume you're sad or hurt when you aren't. Therapists might be digging for some kernel of pain that may have been in their last 99 patients, but is not in you. If you're in touch with how you're really feeling, you can share your state of being with them, even if it's not what they expect to hear. Acknowledge your heart ---- you know yourself best.

48

The same is true for your child. If your child complains that his other parent doesn't seem to love him or care about his feelings because of no visitation or mistreatment during visits, don't downgrade the other parent, but acknowledge the child's true feelings of disappointment and don't make excuses. Encourage the child to be honest with the other parent about his feelings.

4
Friends and Family

**These people can be life savers or saboteurs.
What you can do to get the support you need without
destructive side effects**

49

Your friends and family can be the backbone of your support at this time in your life. If you suddenly decide to quit your job and move to a distant city to get away from the whole situation (and the ex), you may be leaving the only support system you have in place.

50

At the same time, those you care about can do a lot to help or harm your children during the legal process and after. They should never run down the other parent in front of the children. This is still the child's mother or father, due a certain love and respect simply because of that relationship. If that person is a deadbeat, or a liar, or an abuser, the child will learn that on his own as the years pass. Let him keep that idealism ---- we all lose it soon enough.

51

Encourage children's relationships with extended family when it's not harmful. Just as you will always be your child's parent, these people will always be your child's grandparents, aunts, uncles and other relatives. Sometimes when parents are fighting, it's nice for the children to have familiar places they can escape to, with family members to remind them they're loved.

52

If friends offer to take the children for an evening to give you a break, say yes! There seems to be a SuperMan/Woman expectation in our culture which encourages single parents to make martyrs of themselves and prove they can do it all. You deserve to take time for yourself. Make it a weekly gift to you.

53

Often, friends and family members who always disagreed with your choice of partner but who never said so, will be glad to tell you once you've broken up. Give yourself permission to tell them to butt out when you've heard enough.

54

At the same time, take advantage of the opportunity to renew closeness with those who may have grown distant because of conflict with your partner. Get past those petty resentments and rejoin the family!

55

People you know will often encourage you to "get back on the horse" and start dating soon after a breakup. There is no "right" period of time to wait. Some consideration should be given to the legal consequences; ask your attorney if dating will affect any upcoming custody or support matters. If it won't hurt your case, and you feel up to it, go ahead!

56

But, if you don't feel like it, speak up and tell people you're not interested. It's your life. Only you know what progress you're making.

57

If you have a new companion, that person may want to be supportive of you to the point that he or she gets involved in the conflict with your soon-to-be ex, particularly in areas of custody and support. While it's commendable for them to want to help, often just the fact of that person's existence is enough to drive the other party mad. Remember that these are *your* kids. You and the other parent should be the ones discussing any children or money issues. Don't complicate the situation by allowing third parties, however well-intentioned, to interfere in what should be simple negotiations based on what is best for your children.

5
In the Courtroom

**It's unfamiliar territory,
but it doesn't have to be frightening**

58

The courtroom is not nearly as glamorous as what you see on television. Your spouse will not jump up at the last minute under cross-examination and admit he or she had an affair. Perry Mason does not exist.

59

What will happen in the courtroom is like having a painful but necessary surgery without anesthesia. Your life will be uncomfortably cut open, examined, judged, the offending parts removed, the remains sewed back together...and then the healing will begin.

60

The other big fallacy is that the courtroom is about truth and justice. Ask any lawyer, and he'll tell you it's not. It's about who tells the best story. It is up to you to prepare the best 'story' you can, be armed with the best evidence, documents and witnesses, and make the judge see who you are and what your life has been.

61

Nothing can alienate a judge faster than a person who shows disrespect in the courtroom, whether for the judge or the other party. It may be the most difficult thing you've ever done, in the face of what may be blatant lies, not to jump up and shout at the offender, but it is worth the lesson in self-control. You'll be given a chance at the proper time, to answer what is said. You and your attorney need only stay alert for the opportunity to speak.

62

Refrain from little digs at the other party during your testimony; they diminish you in the eyes of the judge or hearing officer.

63

If you're not sure what to expect in court, have your attorney prepare you by conducting a mock hearing, asking you practice questions, both friendly to you, and those you might expect from opposing counsel. Or you could spend a day in court, watching other hearings similar to yours, to see how they are conducted.

In the Courtroom

64

It never hurts to be nice to the court staff. There are plenty of people who are surly and rude to them. Your kind word might well buy you a favor down the road.

65

Your appearance shows your respect for the court. You don't have to dress formally, but remember, this is not the grocery store or the beach. You will win points with the judge by dressing in clean, appropriate clothing. T-shirts with beer slogans on them and jeans with holes will get you a zero.

66

When you're giving and listening to testimony, remember that people's perceptions of an event or series of events may differ. If there's an accident at a street corner, some witnesses will notice the kinds of cars involved, others that there were children in the car, and still others that the light was red. When people tell their stories in court, it will be with those biased perceptions, not necessarily lies, and not necessarily from your point of view. You'll have your chance to tell things the way you saw them.

67

Some hearings are informal; others are formal. Informal hearings are designed to allow lay people to present their own cases, if they so choose. In a formal hearing, there are pieces of evidence or testimony that cannot be offered to the court unless it's done properly. If you have a formal hearing, it is in your best interest to have a skilled attorney by your side, so the court hears everything you want to present. Otherwise, you can count on spending many hours studying the Rules of Evidence and hoping the opposing attorney can't trip you up.

68

The last thing your attorney wants to hear in court for the first time is critical information which damages your case. You might think it's better not to tell your attorney something which might be hard to defend ---- but if she's not prepared, it will hurt your presentation much more, and also jeopardize the relationship between you and your attorney.

6
Support

One of the most hotly-contested court orders, child support is indispensable to custodial parents and misunderstood by those who pay

69

Pay your support.

70

So many times, parents ordered to pay support complain that the money doesn't go to the child. But common sense will tell you that each household only has so much money to go around. If the support check goes to pay the electric bill, then the custodian's paycheck will go for food and housing and toys and clothing. It will all work out by the end of the month.

71

If you find you're having a hard time paying the support that's ordered, the last thing you should be thinking about is taking on more mouths to feed, either by marrying someone or having more children. Those relationships may provide you with temporary love and fulfillment, but the financial picture will only become bleaker.

72

Your children didn't ask to be born. You brought them here. Put your responsibility to them ahead of anything you do for yourself.

73

As much as the court will try to help, realistically speaking, you cannot expect to maintain your previous lifestyle, because two households are inevitably more expensive to maintain than one. As the custodial parent, you may well have to cut back on luxuries you had before, not going to the movies every weekend or for as long a vacation. As the non-custodial parent, you may feel a huge part of your check goes to your ex, and doesn't leave you enough to pay your own bills. Both parents should practice certain economies to give the children the best lives they can.

74

If your children were living with you full-time, you'd spend one quarter to one-third of your income to feed, house, clothe and entertain them. Why should that be different if you live in separate households?

75

It is unfortunate that while the majority of those ordered to pay support pay faithfully, it is the minority who abandon their children who get the news coverage. If you are a custodial parent who gets support regularly, remember to thank the person who's paying once in awhile. He or she will appreciate the recognition.

76

If the person ordered to pay support in your case is not a regular payor, you have certain options through the local child support agency which can help you track that person down and get support. The agencies usually have the ability to run a check for a person through credit bureaus, through the post office, and by social security number and name through the federal parent locator service. You need to know these processes take time, and with caseworkers overloaded by the system, the more information they need to uncover, the longer it will take. While it may seem unfair for you to do the investigating yourself, tracking down the person through relatives, friends or employers, it may well save you aggravation ---- and time ---- in the end.

77

Pay your support. (It bears saying twice.)

7
Property and Finances

Laws regarding property distribution vary from state to state, but handing out the "stuff" is usually very technical

78

The more you fight over 'stuff,' the more money goes out of your pockets and into the pockets of the attorneys.

79

You should stand your ground for what you really deserve, but it's important to keep an eye on the big picture. If you have $20,000 in assets and spend $5,000 for a divorce, you've cut anything you might keep by 25 percent. That's money or property which would be better used to provide for you and your children.

80

The way your property will be divided depends on the laws of your state. If you have a number of assets and debts, it would be a good investment to sit down with a lawyer and receive some advice on those laws, even if you want to make the agreement with your partner directly. This will permit you to make an informed decision based on expert information from an objective third party. You can never have too much information when you are making a financial decision which may affect the rest of your life.

81

In a contested property division, your costs will skyrocket, because everything will have to be appraised, from a calculation of what a pension will be worth at the time of retirement, to the current market value of a house, and even the determination of value of premarital, marital and post marital property. If you can stipulate to the value of even some of the assets, it can save you hundreds of dollars in expert fees.

82

Keep in mind, a settlement agreement or a court order which says that one or the other of the partners is responsible to pay a particular joint debt, such as a credit card, is not enough to get you off the hook if he or she does not pay. You made that original contract with the company, guaranteeing that debt. The only way to make sure your credit's not on the line is to make sure the debt is paid before the divorce is granted.

83

Take any realistic opportunity that is presented to negotiate a settlement, whether through formal mediation or just a sit-down with clients and attorneys. This is your property: the attorneys and judges go home at 5 p.m., but you have a vested interest in these things. You should keep as much control over the process as possible. Once you put your life in the hands of a judge, anything can happen.

84

It is a good policy for both partners to have a general idea of their financial worth: assets and debts, as well as incomes and investments, whether a divorce is contemplated or not. Just because you're not the bill-paying partner doesn't mean you should relinquish all interest in knowing your economic reality. Your partner could be squirreling money away, or running your credit cards up into the tens of thousands without your knowledge, which could have the effect of leaving you at a disadvantage for years to come.

85

It is a sign of the times that the trend is to require both partners to work after the divorce. Even if one of the spouses has been a non-wage earner before this point, he or she should expect to begin contributing financially to his or her own support. Don't let this be a shock to you ---- make plans.

86

When you have a contested property division action before the court, you will be asked to fill out long, detailed lists of the property that exists and explain how it was acquired, whether it was a gift or purchased, and what, if anything, is still owed on it. This paperwork is time-consuming and may involve digging into back records and other files ---- the last thing you feel like doing. But the reason for it is that you and your partner have been unable to agree on the distribution of debt and assets. You have asked total strangers to divide your things for you. You can't expect them to do it fairly without having a complete picture of your situation.

87

At any point during the separation when it looks like financial matters are going to become an issue, get your hands on as much paper as possible ---- copies of year-end pension statements, tax returns, paycheck stubs. Make copies for your own records. These are documents which will become very important, but may be impossible to get after you're out of the house or don't have access to the other party's information.

88

I've had a number of clients who have said, "I don't want anything, I just want out." That's an understandable position, particularly in a situation where there's been emotional or physical abuse. A word of caution: Perhaps what would satisfy you *now* is to escape, but in five years, will you still be as pleased about having nothing? A house, a pension, these are items of joint investment, and it would be to your benefit to think of your life down the road and decide if you want to get your full fair share.

8
Attorneys

Your attorney is someone you hire, just like a plumber or an electrician. Some tips on how to get the most from your professional relationship

89

Your attorney is not your friend. Your attorney is not your mental health counselor. Attorneys are legal professionals skilled in the ways of dissolving relationships through the court system. That's why you pay them. Use their time appropriately.

90

Because you're paying for an attorney's time by the hour, be prepared. Before an appointment with your attorney, take some time to think of the topics you'd like to discuss, and prepare a list of questions. Bring documents which might be useful for copying the first time. Often a written summary or history of particular issues, such as abuse, can be useful. This could be prepared and presented to the attorney for later discussion. Ask the secretary when the appointment is made what might be necessary to bring.

91

Your lawyer counts on what you've promised to pay him or her to feed and house that lawyer's family. Be honest about your ability to pay, pay what you've agreed, and don't promise something you can't deliver. Many attorneys will take a case without a fee; indeed, the ethical rules which bind attorneys demand they do so. But they much prefer to know this at the beginning of a case than at the end.

92

For many people, a divorce is the first time they've had to deal with lawyers. Before deciding which lawyer should represent you, you may have an initial consultation with several, to see which one views the legal process the way you do and which one is willing to pursue your goals, not his or her own agenda.

Attorneys

93

In the same light, expect to find a range of hourly rates and retainers among counsel in your area. What you pay increases with the amount of experience and reputation of the lawyer. Ask about this up front - you don't need surprises.

94

Don't expect your attorney to lie for you. If you've told your attorney you intend to conceal assets, or the attorney finds you have been untruthful about hiding assets, the attorney will likely leave your case. Just be honest.

95

During the process of the divorce, your lawyer may suggest additional legal considerations to you, like a new will designating different beneficiaries, or filing bankruptcy, if your debts are overwhelming. Consider these carefully. You may feel like you're already spending a lot of legal fees on the main matter at hand, but your lawyer has the expertise to see other issues you may miss.

96

If you find you have engaged an attorney who is not representing your interests in the way you'd like, you are allowed to hire a different lawyer. Keep in mind you have a lot of time and money invested in the one you have. The best advice I can give is to set up an appointment with your attorney and speak frankly about your disappointment. It could be that what you're expecting is unrealistic under your circumstances. On the other hand, your attorney may have misunderstood you or be too busy to handle the case as it should be presented

97

If you find that you and your attorney have parted ways, be sensible in the pursuit of another. You can be straightforward with your next choice and tell them what was making you unhappy about your previous arrangement. She may tell you your attorney was right. She may explain how she would do things differently. Either way, you'll have to start over with the new attorney, in terms of providing her with information. It will cost you a little more, but might well leave you closer to where you wanted to be by the end of the process.

98

Often clients ask me if it's necessary for their spouse to get another attorney, or if they can both use the same one. They're trying to save on legal fees. The ethical problem which develops is that an attorney is supposed to zealously advocate for his client. It may be that you and your spouse have opposing interests; how could the same attorney fight hard for each of you against the other? If everything is agreed down to the last detail, maybe it will work. But you don't want to tie his hands before he even gets started.

99

Another situation which comes up infrequently is that a divorce becomes personal to the attorney; either the attorney becomes Don Quixote, crusading to save the client in a dramatic (and perhaps unnecessary) way, or the other party decides to take on the attorney because of a personal dislike. These people have lost sight of the issue. If the attorney becomes the issue, then it is time for that attorney to step out of the case and let someone else handle it.

100

If you feel you need an attorney, but you don't have the funds, don't give up. You have a number of options. It is possible to get the other party to pay for your attorney and your costs, if they have the means. There are also attorneys who will handle these matters at no cost to you; you can find them by contacting the local Court administrator or Bar Association and asking for a referral. Be persistent ---- it's your right.

9
After It's Over

**Your new life will never be the same,
but that doesn't mean it can't be better**

101

Take a deep breath. It's probably been one of the most difficult periods of your life, even if it's something you chose. If you have children, you're realizing that you're still tied to their other parent after the divorce, at least until they're 18, and probably on through graduations, weddings, and even grandchildren. (But take heart —— many find after the pressure cooker of the breakup is done they can become civil again, at least for the sake of their children.) There are final documents to sign, deeds to draw and record, pensions to be collected, houses to be closed up and sold. That life is done.

One door closes behind; another opens ahead. How you spend the rest of your life is up to you. Empower yourself to say "Yes!" to all that awaits, and step through that door. You have survived. Be well. Tread your road gladly, armed with the lessons you've learned. Be good to yourself.

www.divorcesource.com

www.divorcesupport.com

These two sites are linked together and provide a mega-site with information dating from 1997-98, with links for fathers and mothers rights, domestic violence links, a list of publications for more information, bulletin boards and chats.

www.Divorcecentral.com

Good listing of FAQs about divorce and separation...along with a resource guide, message boards and chat.

http://divorcesupport.miningco.com

Newsletter format with articles and links to assorted divorce topics.

www.parentsplace.com/readroom

Parentsplace has a huge amount of information for parents ---- single or not, and links to various sites with single parent information.

www.divorceonline.com

Interesting site with online access to multi-disciplinary professionals ---- lawyers, accountant and therapists, for advice and Q&A.

http://divorcenet.com

This site has a number of chat support groups, an attorney resource center, and a listing of state by state legal provisions, as well as bulletin board discussion on a number of topics.

www.dudley-gateway.co.uk/cz/czindex.htm

This is a site for kids to e-mail a counselor and talk...some of the Q&A are posted. Most of the information and resources are England- based.

Parents Without Partners

www.parentswithoutpartners.org

This group is generally acknowledged to be the granddaddy of support groups, mainly catering to divorced men and women when it first began in the late 1950s. There is a resource center open to all, as well as a directory of local chapters and a search device to help anyone find a chapter near them. A listing of local and international PWP events makes it easy for people to find out how they can get involved.

http://home.navisoft.com/solemom/index.htm

Sole Mothers International is a site that means business, putting a host of resources at the tips of the single parent's fingers. Experts await individual questions, "Operation: Net Support" places single parents in touch with child support enforcement agencies, and legal information from across the country is available with a single click.

Sites b y Individuals:

www.nucleus.com/~jlassali

Single Parents World, maintained by Jill Lassaline. This is one of the best sites I found for a list of links where everyone can find information relevant to his/her situation. Jill's page has links to the Single Fathers Lighthouse, Sole Mothers Resource, the Single Dad's Index, PWP, Single Mothers by Choice, and much more, in addition to her own personal observations.

http://rampages.onramp.net/~bevhamil/singleparentresourcece_478.html

Single Parent Resource Center, maintained by Beverly Hamilton

Beverly is a single parent from Texas who compiled this list of 19 links when she was searching for information and support during her own unexpected divorce. The amount of excellent information here is stunning, complete with legal resources on every topic from collecting child support through divorce, custody and how to choose a lawyer. There are lists of sites offering support to single moms, and others for single dads, organizations and publications to help single parents, and religious sources of all persuasions for those seeking a little outside guidance when times get tough.

Index

RebuildingBooks
For Divorce and Beyond

50 WAYS TO LOVE YOUR LEAVER
Getting on With Your Life After the Breakup

Dwight Webb, Ph.D.

Softcover: $14.95   176 pages

Psychologist's sensitive, compassionate, insightful guide offers hope and encouragement to those in despair at the end of an intimate relationship. Covers grief, intimacy and loss, denial, letting go of blame and anger, much more.

REBUILDING
When Your Relationship Ends (Second Edition)

Bruce Fisher, Ed.D.

Softcover: $12.95   336 pages

The most popular guide to divorce recovery. The "divorce process rebuilding blocks" format offers a nineteen-step process for putting life back together after divorce. Includes material on adaptation, fear, openness, relatedness and purpose. Built on two decades of research and practice. More than half a million in print.

DIVORCE HANDBOOK FOR CALIFORNIA (Fourth Edition)
How to Dissolve Your Marriage Without Disaster

Judge James W. Stewart

Softcover: $19.95   208 pages

Family court judge shows how to establish realistic expectations about divorce; find and hire a good attorney; control attorney's actions and fees; use mediation and/or arbitration; handle child and spousal support; protect children.

Since 1970 — Psychology you can use, from professionals you can trust

Impact 🕮 Publishers®, Inc.

Post Office Box 6016, Atascadero, California 93423-6016
Orders 800-246-7228 • Phone 805-466-5917 • Fax 805-466-5919 • E-mail info@impactpublishers.com • Web at www.impactpublishers.com